Cake Decorating
for the first time®

Cake Decorating
for the first time®

Jaynie Maxfield

Sterling Publishing Co., Inc.
New York
A Sterling/Chapelle Book

Chapelle Ltd.

Jo Packham
Sara Toliver
Cindy Stoeckl

Editor: Karmen Quinney
Editorial Director: Caroll Shreeve
Art Director: Karla Haberstich
Copy Editor: Marilyn Goff
Graphic Illustrator: Kim Taylor
Photography: Kevin Dilley for Hazen Photography
Photo Stylist: Jaynie Maxfield
Staff: Burgundy Alleman, Kelly Ashkettle, Areta Bingham, Ray Cornia, Emily Frandsen, Lana Hall, Susan Jorgensen, Barbara Milburn, Lecia Monsen, Suzy Skadburg, Desirée Wybrow

Library of Congress Cataloging-in-Publication Data

Cake decorating for the first time/Jaynie Maxfield.
    p. cm.
ISBN 1-4027-0538-7
1. Cake decorating. I. Title.
TX771.2.M38 2003
641.8'653--dc21
                                        2003006878

10 9 8 7 6 5 4 3 2 1

Published by Sterling Publishing Co., Inc.
387 Park Avenue South, New York, NY 10016
©2003 by Jaynie Maxfield
Distributed in Canada by Sterling Publishing
c/o Canadian Manda Group, One Atlantic Avenue, Suite 105
Toronto, Ontario, Canada M6K 3E7
Distributed in Great Britain by Chrysalis Books
64 Brewery Road, London N7 9NT, England
Distributed in Australia by Capricorn Link (Australia) Pty. Ltd.
P.O. Box 704, Windsor, NSW 2756, Australia
Printed in China
All Rights Reserved

Sterling ISBN 1-4027-0538-7

Write Us

If you have any questions or comments, please contact:
Chapelle, Ltd., Inc.,
P.O. Box 9252, Ogden, UT 84409
(801) 621-2777 • (801) 621-2788 Fax
e-mail: chapelle@chapelleltd.com
web site: chapelleltd.com

The more you bake, the better you will become; and when you are stuck, remember it is only food—and you are smarter than food. So put in the time, let yourself learn, and start having fun.

Table of Contents

Section 4:
Gallery—94

Introduction

Section 1: Cake Decorating Basics familiarizes you with the basic tools and supplies you need to begin.

Section 2: Basic Techniques contains instructions for eight techniques that can be made using basic cake-decorating techniques.

Section 3: Beyond the Basics expands on the techniques learned in Section 2 with eight additional projects that are a bit more complex.

Section 4: Gallery features beautifully decorated cakes and advanced cake-decorating skills.

The purpose of *Cake Decorating for the first time*® is to provide a starting point that teaches basic skills. It will inspire you to make a special cake dessert for a dinner party or the ultimate—a wedding cake.

Ideas can come from china, fabrics, or events. Take time to develop the basic techniques, then create your own wonderful cakes. The more you practice, the more comfortable you will feel. Allow yourself reasonable time to decorate your first cake— remember this is your first time. You will soon discover that the techniques are easy to master.

After you complete the first few projects, you will be surprised by how quickly you will be able to finish the remaining cakes. Take pride in the talents you are developing and the unique and memorable decorated cakes that only you can create.

HOW TO USE THIS BOOK

A wide variety of decorated cakes are shown in this book. Feel free to change colors, shapes, and sizes of my cake examples to suit your design tastes and ideas.

Various skills are taught in this book. Learning these techniques and how to apply them will inspire you to invent and decorate beautiful cakes of your own.

To decorate each cake, you will need a few essential items, a well-baked cake, and time to master the basic techniques. As each one is explained, enjoy practicing until you feel confident to attempt multiple layers and more elaborate trims.

Plan extra time for baking several cakes for tiered projects. Filled and fancifully trimmed cakes may also have more steps. Soon, you will master skills that have you serving your own fabulous cakes.

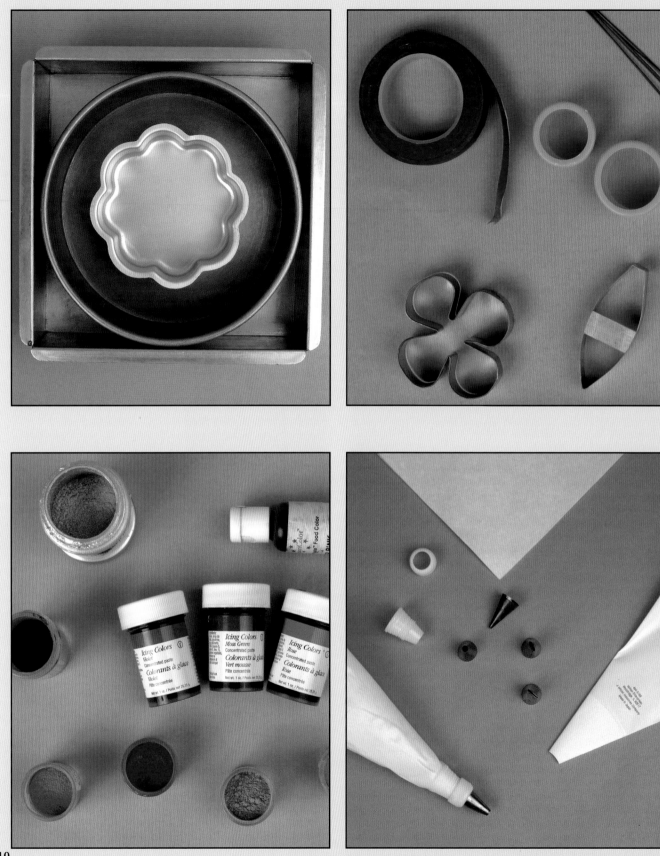

Section 1: Cake Decorating Basics

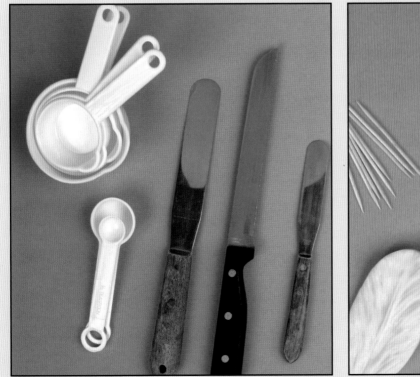

What do I need to get started?

To achieve the perfectly decorated cake, it is important to have the correct equipment from the pans to the oven temperature. No matter how beautifully a cake is decorated, if the beginning product—the cake—is inferior, then the decorations will not look right. Most of the necessary equipment you will probably already have in your kitchen—basic items like measuring cups, measuring spoons, mixing bowls, a stovetop, an oven, and a mixer.

A mixer with attached bowl as shown below is recommend over a hand-mixer. It makes the job easier and handles large quantities of batter and icing. A turntable is also highly recommended. It makes the job of decorating much easier.

CAKE PANS

Square Pan

Round Pan

Shaped Pan

There are many options in bakeware available today. For dependable baking success, it is important to invest in sturdy cake pans. Cake pans come in divers shapes and sizes, and are made from various materials. Heavy aluminum cake pans work the best. They can withstand rough handling, high oven temperatures, and will not rust.

Additionally, it is important to bake with pans that are in good condition. Make certain cake pans are not warped or pitted.

When selecting a cake pan, be aware that pan diameters vary. Always use the size and type of cake pans specified in the recipe. Standard cake pans, no matter what the pan diameter, are usually 1½"–2" high on the sides. I prefer 3"-high pans because you get more volume out of your batter. Cake pans are available in hundreds of shapes from hearts to cartoon characters. Round, square, and rectangular cake pans are the most common.

GENERAL UTENSILS

Dry Measuring Cups

Measuring Spoons

Metal Spatula

Serrated-edged Knife

Metal Spatula

Rubber Spatula

Large Metal Spoon

Wire Whisk

Wooden Spoon

Dry Measuring Cups—used to measure dry ingredients.

Measuring Spoons—used to measure small portions of dry and liquid ingredients.

Metal Spatulas—used to apply icing to the cake. They are available in various sizes. The larger the cake, the larger the necessary spatula.

Serrated-edged Knife—used for leveling cakes, cutting cakes, and other miscellaneous duties.

Rubber Spatula—used for folding in lightweight ingredients and for scraping batter, icing, and fillings from bowls.

Large Metal Spoon—used to stir large amounts of ingredients together and to remove large amounts of fondant and gum paste from the bowl.

Wire Whisk—used to fold ingredients together.

Wooden Spoon—used to stir ingredients together.

Decorative Cake Plate

Corrugated Cardboard Cake Rounds

Acrylic Cake Plate

Turntable

A cake plate is any display surface on which you wish to place a cake. It can be your favorite china plate, a cake stand, a piece of cardboard covered with aluminum foil, or a cake round purchased at your local craft store. The most important thing about a cake plate is that it is large enough to hold and support the weight of the cake. Cake plates can be garnished to be hidden, if so desired. The following are a few cake plate options:

Decorative Cake Plate—can be any plate in your kitchen on which the cake will fit. You may use plate styles from china to everyday ware.

Turntables—come in various sizes and styles. They range in price from under $10.00 to $80.00. Turntables make cake decorating easier by giving more maneuverability while working around the cake.

Corrugated Cardboard Cake Rounds—come in various sizes and styles and offer strength and stability for your cake. Cake rounds can be purchased at your local craft store. They are available with ruffled edges or scalloped edges and come in white, silver foil, or gold foil. Cake rounds can also be ordered in other foil colors through speciality cake stores. They are inexpensive and can be discarded.

Corrugated Cardboard Cake Boards (not shown)—come in various sizes and offer strength and stability for your cake. Because of their rectangular shape, they work well for square and sheet cakes. They are inexpensive and can be discarded.

Acrylic Cake Plates—are custom-made acrylic surfaces. They are sturdy and versatile. Acrylic cake plates disappear into the setting in which the cake is placed.

PASTRY BAGS & DECORATING TIPS

Pastry bags and decorating tips are used to create piping on a cake, such as icing flowers, borders, and lettering.

Pastry Bags—come in three styles: reusable, disposable, and parchment. Each style is unique and has its distinct advantages.

The reusable pastry bags come in a variety of sizes are made from canvas, nylon, plastic, plastic-lined cotton, and polyester. They are specially coated to prevent leaks. They are also very flexible to work with when decorating a cake. They are washable and made to be reused.

The disposable pastry bags are made from clear plastic. They are handy for fast decorating and easy cleanup. However, they are not as flexible as reusable pastry bags and parchment triangles.

Parchment triangles come in different sizes and are folded to create pastry bags. They work best when using small amounts of icing. Couplers are not used on parchment triangles.

Couplers—come in two sizes and make it easy to interchange decorating tips on a pastry bag without changing the bag. If you do not use a coupler, a new bag must be prepared for each new tip. Couplers are a two-part device, consisting of a base that slips inside the bag and a ring that secures onto the base and bag from the outside.

Decorating Tips—come in a variety of styles and sizes. They are small metal cones that fit into or on a pastry bag. The size of the tip and the angle in which it is held while decorating will determine the look of the decoration. There are hundreds of tips in various shapes and sizes. They range in price from 80 cents to $2.00 each.

Leaf tips have v-shaped openings to create leaves with center veins. The most commonly used leaf tips are #65, #67, and #352.

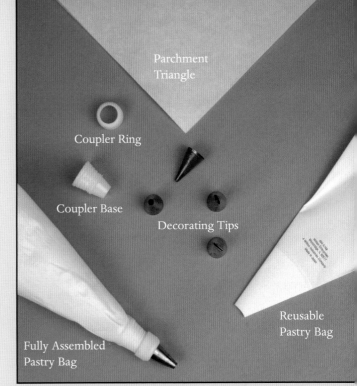

Parchment Triangle

Coupler Ring

Coupler Base

Decorating Tips

Reusable Pastry Bag

Fully Assembled Pastry Bag

Rose tips have slanted openings to create rose petals, rosebuds, ruffles, and bows. The most commonly used rose tips are #101, #102, #104, #124, and #127.

Round tips have round openings used for lettering, fine-detail work, and outlines.

Star tips have star-shaped openings and are the most popular tips used because they create just about everything from star borders to rosettes. The most commonly used star tips are #14, #16, #18, #32, and #199.

To clean-up pastry bags after use, remove coupler ring and tip from bag, using a spoon to scrape out the icing. If the pastry bag is disposable or made from a parchment triangle, simply throw it away. For a reusable pastry bag, turn the bag inside out, wash with hot water and dishwashing liquid, then allow to dry. It is not recommended that you place a reusable pastry bag in the dishwasher, the high-temperature drying can cause the bag to melt.

What do I need to know about food coloring?

Food coloring is used to tint icing, gum paste, and fondant. Food coloring is available in four forms: gel, liquid, paste, and powder. Remember when working with any food coloring that it is a dye and will stain porous surfaces, hands, and clothing. Handle with care.

Gel Food Coloring (not shown)—comes in a variety of colors and blends easily.

Liquid Food Coloring—comes in a variety of colors and is the weakest of the four types of food coloring. This works best in coloring cake batter, breads, and other baked items.

Paste Food Coloring—comes in a variety of colors and creates vivid and deep hues for gum paste, icing, and fondant.

Powdered Food Coloring—comes in a variety of colors, will not bleed, and has no taste. It is used for icing and fondant.

Gold & Silver Powder Dusts—are used to enhance gum paste or fondant. Mix a small amount of almond extract in gold and silver powder to paint on fondant or dried gum paste.

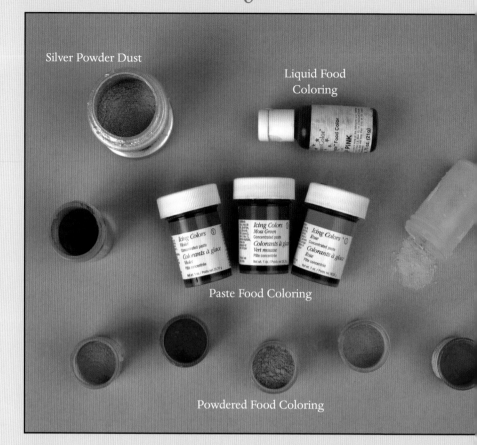

Silver Powder Dust

Liquid Food Coloring

Paste Food Coloring

Powdered Food Coloring

Tips:

• When using food coloring, the finished product should always look natural and appetizing.

• Dark colors should be used in small amounts.

• Colored icing will darken as it dries.

• When kneading food coloring into fondant, place a light coat of shortening on your hands to keep them from getting too badly stained.

• Experiment with the different types of food colorings to find which type you like best.

What equipment do I need to decorate with fondant?

To create a fondant-iced cake, additional equipment will be needed. The following items are a must when learning how to decorate a cake with fondant:

Pizza Cutter—used to trim excess fondant from cake edges. It is much easier to use than pastry scissors or a knife.

Rolling Pin—used to roll out fondant to ¼" thickness on work surface. The rolling pin is also used to transport the fondant from the work surface to the cake and aids in draping the fondant over the cake.

Smoother—used to smooth the fondant.

Tape Measure (not shown)—used to measure the diameter and height of a cake. Measuring the cake helps ensure the correct amount of fondant will be rolled out to cover the cake.

Pizza Cutter

Smoother

Rolling Pin

What equipment do I need to create gum–paste florals?

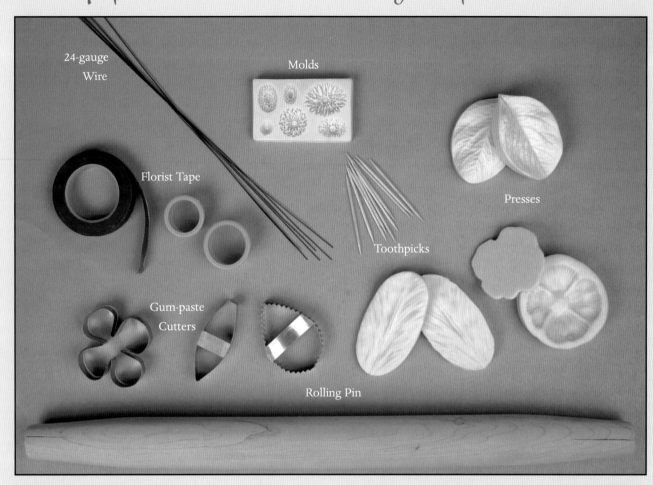

24-gauge
Wire

Molds

Florist Tape

Presses

Toothpicks

Gum-paste
Cutters

Rolling Pin

To create gum-paste decorations, additional equipment will be needed. The following items are equipment used to decorate the gum-paste decorations in this book:

24-gauge Wire—inserted into gum-paste florals to create stems to give them lift on the cake.

Florist Tape—used to attach individual gum-paste decorations together.

Gum-paste Cutters—come in various sizes and styles. They are used to create shapes from rolled gum paste.

Molds—come in various shapes and sizes. Molds are used to create texture and to shape items from gum paste.

Toothpicks—act as a handle and for attaching flower center to petals.

Presses—come in various shapes and sizes. Presses are used to create the details in gum-paste shapes.

Rolling Pin—used to roll out gum paste.

SUCCESSFUL CAKE DECORATING TIPS:

- Tie back long hair, clean under fingernails, avoid wearing fuzzy clothing, and remove any jewelry on your hands and wrists. Also, use a lint roller or masking tape to remove any lint or hair from clothing.

- Allow ingredients to acclimate to room temperature.

- Assemble all necessary equipment.

- Make certain equipment and work surface are clean.

- Always preheat oven.

- Grease and flour bottoms of pans only. *Note: I do not recommend butter because it is more easily absorbed into the batter and it is more expensive to use.*

- Alway sift flour. After sifting, measure flour by spooning into measuring cup. Level with knife. Resift with salt and leavening ingredient. *Note: Not sifting flour can result in more flour than necessary. It is important to use cake flour when specified and all-purpose flour when specified.*

- Use the best ingredients you can afford.

- Use the freshest ingredients you can buy.

- Separate eggs while they are cold.

- Alternate dry and wet ingredients when making your batter. Begin and end with flour mixture.

- Using mixer, beat egg whites until soft peaks are formed. Using wire whisk, fold lightly into batter, folding in the same direction until incorporated to keep air in whites.

- Fill pans ½ full to allow room for cakes to rise.

- Bake the cake immediately after mixing, as near the center of the oven as possible.

- Place pans in oven, making certain pans do not touch, so air can circulate and cakes can bake evenly. Open oven door as little as possible.

- Allow cakes to cool on a cooling rack before removing from pan.

Section 2: Techniques

1
technique

Equipment:
Cake plate
Flour
Heavy aluminum saucepan
Measuring cups: dry; liquid
Measuring spoons
Mixer w/bowl
Mixing bowls
Rubber spatula
Shortening
Sifter
Square cake pans: 8" (2)
Stovetop/oven
Thin-edged knife

How do I bake a cake?

It is important to have recipes that will bake moist, medium- to heavy-bodied cakes—especially for a beginner because they are easier to ice.

Chocolate Cake—*Here's How:*

MAKING & BAKING

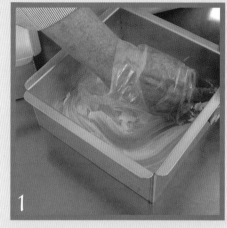

1. Preheat oven to 350°. Grease bottom of pan with shortening.

2. Flour bottom of pan. Holding pan upside down, tap out excess flour.

3. Sift first four dry ingredients into mixing bowl.

4. Stir margarine, oil, water, and cocoa together in saucepan.

5. Heat on low until melted.

Chocolate Cake:

2½ cups all-purpose flour, sifted
1 teaspoon salt
1 teaspoon baking soda
¼ cup cinnamon
1 stick margarine
4 ounces vegetable oil
1 cup water
⅓ cup cocoa
4 ounces buttermilk
2 eggs
⅓ cup applesauce
2 cups sugar

6. Mix buttermilk, eggs, and applesauce together.

7. Add sifted ingredients to egg mixture. Beat until all lumps are gone.

TIPS:

• Add sifted ingredients slowly, not dump in all at once.

• Cool cake on level cooling rack before removing from pan.

• Do not rush the processes of baking and decorating. Allow plenty of time for both.

8. Using rubber spatula, slowly stir cocoa mixture into batter.

9. Pour batter into greased and floured pan, filling only ½ full.

Alternative Recipe:

Lemon Cake:

2 cups cake flour
2 teaspoons baking powder
¾ teaspoon salt
1 cup sugar
½ cup shortening
¾ cup milk
3 egg whites
¼ cup sugar
1 teaspoon lemon extract

MAKING & BAKING

1. Sift together the first four ingredients. Place in mixer. Add shortening and milk. Mix well.

2. Beat egg whites until stiff. Add ¼ cup of sugar and beat until meringue forms.

3. Fold meringue into batter, gently beating in an over-and-under manner.

4. Add extract. Mix well.

5. Bake at 350° for 20 minutes or until done. Using thin-edged knife, test center of cake. Remove cake from oven when knife comes out clean.

10. Bake 40 minutes or until done. Using thin-edged knife, test center of cake. Remove the cake from oven when the knife comes out clean.

11. Make certain cake is cool to the touch. Using thin-edged knife, remove cake from pan by running knife around edges of cake pan. Make certain to avoid cutting the cakes. *Note: The natural edge on the cakes helps them hold their shape and makes it much easier to ice.*

12. Using serrated-edged knife, remove any high spots and level off top. *Note: Make certain not to remove too much. You can always remove more if necessary.*

13. Place cake on cake plate.

How do I decorate a cake without icing?

Powdered sugar is a great and easy way to decorate a cake. Powdered sugar can be easily sifted onto the cake or it can be sifted onto a design template. When using a design template, remember it works best with very simple designs.

Equipment:
Mortar / pestle (optional)
Resealable plastic bag
Round cake pans: 8" (2)
Template: desired design

Equipment for Chocolate Cake
on page 22

Colored Powdered Sugar:

1 cup powdered sugar
1 teaspoon powdered food coloring

Powdered-sugar Motif—*Here's How:*

MAKING & BAKING

1. Make and bake two 8" Chocolate Cakes. See Chocolate Cake on page 23. Refer to Technique 1, Steps 1–13 on pages 22–24.

2. Place powdered food coloring and powdered sugar in a plastic bag. Seal and shake.

DECORATING

1. Center and place template on the cake.

2. Place colored powdered sugar into sifter. Sift onto template to desired thickness.

3. Carefully remove template.

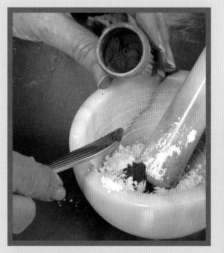

Note: A mortar and pestle can be used to blend food coloring and powdered sugar.

TIPS:

- To lighten the colored powdered sugar, add more powdered sugar.

- To darken the colored powdered sugar, add more food coloring.

- Use a child's snowflake, valentine heart, or other simple cut-out design as your template.

- Cut your first or last name out of paper and use as your template.

- Use a cookie cutter, lace doily, or a pressed leaf as a template.

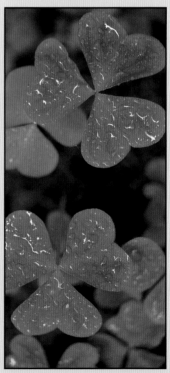

How do I ice a cake?

The most important thing about icing a cake is the temperature of the icing. Make certain the icing is warm enough to manipulate without being runny. There are several ways to ice a cake. Each can be easily mastered. Icing seals in the moisture and flavor of the cake. Always crumb-coat the cake before decorating with icing.

3
technique

Equipment:
Candy thermometer
Metal spatula
Refrigerator

Equipment for Chocolate
Cake on page 22

Buttercream Icing:
1 pound softened butter
4 pounds powdered sugar
2 teaspoons vanilla
1 teaspoon salt
1 cup egg whites
1 cup sugar
½ cup water

MAKING
1. In saucepan, bring sugar and water to 212° on stovetop.

2. In mixing bowl, combine butter, two pounds of powdered sugar, vanilla, salt, and egg whites.

3. Alternate adding boiled sugar water with remaining powdered sugar into icing mixture.

Iced Cake—*Here's How:*

MAKING & BAKING

1. Make and bake two 8" Chocolate Cakes. See Chocolate Cake on page 23. Refer to Technique 1, Steps 1–13 on pages 22–24.

CRUMB COATING

1. Crumb-coat cake, using the following technique:

   a. Brush off any crumbs from first cake.

   b. Using metal spatula, apply icing to top of first cake. *Note: Fruit fillings can be used instead of icing, such as raspberry, strawberry, apricot, etc. Caramel, butterscotch sauce, and chocolate fillings such as Chocolate Butter-cream Icing and Ganache can also be used.*

   c. Place second cake upside down on top of first cake. Brush off any crumbs from cake.

   d. Using metal spatula, apply a thin layer of icing to top first, then sides. If necessary, thin icing by warming in microwave.

2. After cake is completely covered, refrigerate cake for 30 minutes or until cold.

FOR COLORED ICING

1. Place desired amount of icing in bowl.

2. Tint icing, using one of the following methods:

b2. Wipe knife or toothpick into icing. *Note: Do not place butter knife or toothpick back into paste. This will ruin the color and cause it to become moldy.*

a. For powdered food coloring, sprinkle a small amount of coloring into icing.

c. For liquid food coloring, place a drop or two into icing.

3. Using spoon, stir until thoroughly blended. Do not add more food coloring until blended.

b1. For paste food coloring, load a small amount of coloring onto a knife or toothpick.

TIPS:

- Choose colors that will look natural and carry the theme of the cake.

- Mix more tinted icing of each color than you think you will need. It is difficult to tint the exact same color twice.

- Hold some untinted icing in reserve to lighten dark icing.

- Place only a small amount of food coloring in icing. Remember, more food coloring can always be added. If you happen to tint the icing darker than desired, remove half the icing and add some of the untinted icing held in reserve and blend.

- To help darken icing, paint inside of pastry bag with food coloring and a paintbrush.

- Use separate mixing bowls and spoons for each color of icing.

- Cover bowls containing icing with a damp cloth or plastic wrap so the icing will not dry out.

Alternative Recipe:

Chocolate Icing:

⅔ cup butter, softened
4 cups powdered sugar
3 to 5 tablespoons milk
1 teaspoon vanilla
⅓ cup unsweetened cocoa

MIXING

1. In large bowl, cream butter until light and fluffy.

2. Blend cocoa into creamed butter.

3. Gradually add powdered sugar, beating well after each addition.

4. Add milk and vanilla. Beat until blended.

FOR SMOOTH ICING

1. Smooth icing onto chilled cake, using the following method:

   a. Using metal spatula, apply second coat of icing to cake.

   b. Dip metal spatula into hot water. Always shake off excess water.

   c. Stroke icing, starting on cake top. Dip metal spatula into hot water and shake before every stroke.

   d. Repeat until smooth on cake top.

2. Repeat Step 1b–d on sides and seam.

FOR SWIRLED ICING

1. Swirl icing, using the following technique:

1a

a. Using metal spatula, apply a second coat of icing to cake, making c-shaped motions in icing on top of cake.

1b

b. Step back to view cake.

1c

c. Add more c shapes, if necessary.

2

2. Repeat Step 1a–c on sides.

Alternative Recipe:

Cloud Icing:

2 egg whites
¼ teaspoon salt
1½ teaspoons vanilla
¼ cup sugar
¾ cup light corn syrup

MAKING

1. Beat egg whites, salt, and vanilla in mixer over medium speed until foamy.

2. Gradually add sugar, beating at highest speed until soft peaks form and sugar is dissolved.

3. In small saucepan, bring corn syrup to a boil over medium heat. Remove from heat and pour corn syrup over sugar mixture, beating at highest speed until mixture is stiff.

How do I create a simple decorated cake?

Since food is not a perfect thing, simple decorations can help to hide imperfections in the cake itself or in the icing. Items such as coconut, fresh flowers, fruit, or candy can turn a simple iced cake into a lovely centerpiece. Look around your kitchen and see what you have. Make it fun. Make it unique.

Simple Decorated Cake—*Here's How:*

MAKING & BAKING

1. Make and bake two 8" Chocolate Cakes. See Chocolate Cake on page 23. Refer to Technique 1, Step 1–13 on pages 22–24.

2. Make Buttercream Icing. See Buttercream Icing on page 27.

3. Crumb-coat cake. Refer to Crumb Coating, Steps 1–2 on page 28.

4. Smooth-ice cake. Refer to For Smooth Icing, Steps 1–2 on page 30.

5. Decorate cake. See desired simple decorated cake instructions on pages 33–35.

FOR COCONUT LEMON CAKE

1. Using fingers, break up any coconut clumps.

2. Sprinkle coconut on cake top and cake plate.

3. Using paring knife and cutting board, cut desired number of lemon slices from lemon. Cut each lemon slice ¾ of the way through.

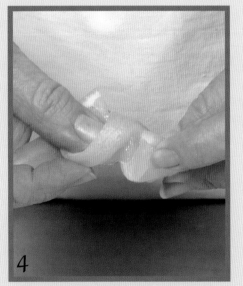

4. Twist lemon ends in opposite direction. Place on cake top.

TIPS:

- Creatively arrange simple food items on the iced-cake.

  Following are some simple ideas:
  Blueberries
  Caramel syrup
  Cherries
  Chocolate candies
  Crushed cookies
  Grated candy bar
  Orange slices
  Jelly beans
  Kiwi
  Lime slices
  Peppermint candies
  Pineapple slices
  Raisins
  Raspberries
  Strawberries

- Place favorite cookie cutter on iced cake as desired. Remove, then fill in design with chopped nuts or colored powdered sugar. See Powdered-sugar Motif on pages 25–26.

33

TIPS:

• Decorate cake with edible flowers. Make certain to check with your florist on flowers that are edible.

• Before cutting cake, remove daisies. Cut cake and place pieces on serving plates. Embellish each piece of cake with one or two daisies. *Note: If necessary, use the extra daisies in vase for embellishing individual pieces of cake.*

FOR DAISY CAKE

1. Using scissors, cut desired number of daisy stems 2" in length. *Note: Place any remaining daisies in a vase filled with water and use as decoration next to the cake.*

2. Insert daisies into cake as desired.

FOR CHOCOLATE CURL CAKE

  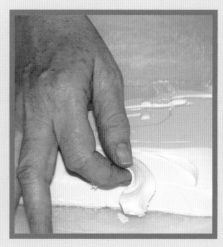

1. Warm white chocolate under a lamp for six hours.

2. Using vegetable peeler, curl white chocolate.

Note: If the white chocolate is too warm it will not curl.

Chocolate curls can also be created from dark chocolate. Chocolate curls can be thick or thin. Their shape will vary depending on how much is curled at one time.

5
technique

Equipment:
Decorating tips
Parchment triangles: 15"
Pastry bag coupler/ring
Tablespoon

Equipment for Chocolate Cake
on page 22

Equipment for Iced Cake
on page 27

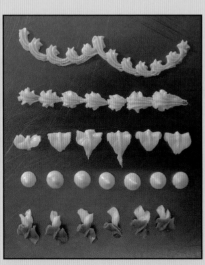

Think of the tip on the pastry bag as the point of a pen and begin practicing your penmanship. If you make a mistake do not worry, simply remove the design and start again.

How do I decorate a cake using a pastry bag and decorating tips?

Piping is a popular way to decorate a cake. Piping is done with a pastry bag. A pastry bag is fitted with the desired decorating tip on the small end and filled with icing in the large end. The tip is used to create designs called piping. Learning to control the pastry bag will take some time and practice, but the final results will be worth it.

Piped Decorated Cake—

Here's How:

MAKING & BAKING

1. Make and bake two 8" Chocolate Cakes. See Chocolate Cake on page 23. Refer to Technique 1, Steps 1–13 on pages 22–24.

2. Crumb-coat cake. Refer to Crumb Coating, Steps 1–2 on page 28.

3. Smooth-ice cake. Refer to For Smooth Icing, Steps 1–2 on page 30.

ASSEMBLING PASTRY BAG

1. Place parchment triangle on work surface. *Note: Center of long edge will become the point of the pastry bag.*

2. Roll left point of parchment triangle up to top-center point.

Alternative Equipment:

If you prefer to use a reusable pastry bag or a plastic disposable pastry bag, refer to Steps 5–6 on page 38 then squeeze outside of bag, pushing icing to bottom of pastry bag toward tip. Fold down top of bag to secure, then continue with Steps 9–10 on page 38.

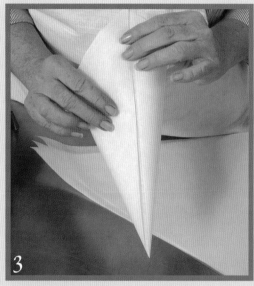

3. Hold roll in place with thumb. Roll right point around first roll and up to top-center to make pastry bag.

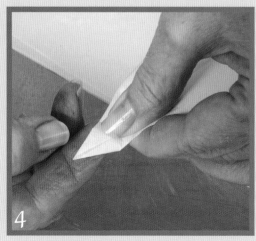

4. Tear ½" off bottom point.

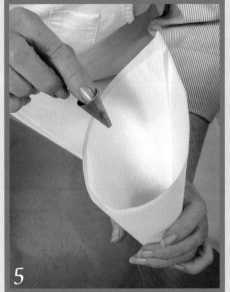

5. Drop desired decorating tip into pastry bag. *Note: If using a coupler, drop coupler base into top of pastry bag down through torn end until one or two threads show through the hole. Attach tip and coupler ring to threads of coupler base.*

6. Spoon desired icing into pastry bag, filling only ½ way.

7. Squeeze outside of paper, pushing icing to bottom of pastry bag toward tip.

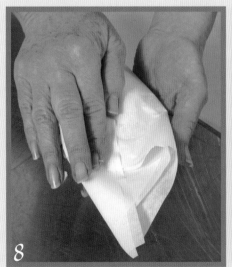

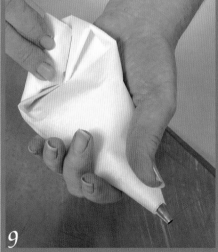

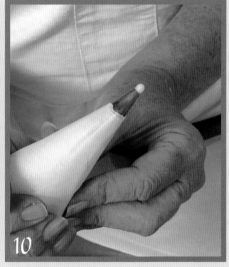

8. Fold right edge over, then left edge over, closing bag. *Note: It is important to close off bag so icing does not leak out.*

9. Fold down top of bag to secure.

10. Squeeze a small amount of icing into icing bowl, making certain there are no air bubbles in pastry bag. Air in pastry bag will disrupt the design. *Note: This should be done every time a pastry bag is filled with icing.*

USING PASTRY BAG & DECORATING TIPS

Individual Decorations

1. Practice on work surface before applying to cake.

2. Place tip on cake and squeeze pastry bag with right hand, using index finger on left hand as guide for tip. It is important to be able to apply steady pressure with your entire hand. The decoration will be affected by the amount of pressure applied to bag. *Note: Reverse for left-handers.*

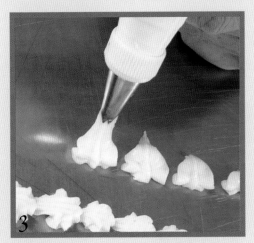

3. Pull straight up.

4. Continue until desired design or border is complete.

TIPS:

- Practice using tips at different angles for desired look. Holding the bag at a 90 degree angle works well for creating flat flowers and stars. Holding the bag at a 45 degree angle works well for borders and writing.

- Remember to raise the tip as the icing mounts or a depression will form in the icing.

- If a pastry bag has been sitting unused, the icing on the tip will most likely become crusted. A toothpick may need to be inserted into the tip to remove any dried icing before piping again. Try keeping pastry bags under a damp cloth.

- Use a different color of icing to accent the piped decoration.

- For a variegated icing, stripe inside of pastry bag with ½"-wide stripe of paste food coloring the same color as the icing that will be used. Fill bag with icing.

Continual Decorations

1. Practice on work surface before applying to cake.

2. Place tip on cake or work surface and squeeze pastry bag with right hand, using index finger on left hand as a guide for tip. *Note: Reverse for left-handers.*

3. Apply pressure consistently when creating a continual decoration. When decoration is complete, pull straight off. *Note: The decoration will be affected by the amount of pressure applied to bag and the steadiness of the pressure.*

TIPS:

• Using toothpick, write desired message on waxed paper. Place waxed paper on top of dry iced cake. Using toothpick, prick around the message, going through the waxed paper. Remove waxed paper. Using pastry bag and desired tip, pipe over tiny holes in the icing.

• Decorating tip should lightly touch the cake while writing.

• When reaching the end of a continuous decoration, stop squeezing before pulling straight off.

These continual decorations were created by repeating an individual design. Remember holding the bag at different angles and the movement of your hand will result in completely different-looking decorations.

DECORATING

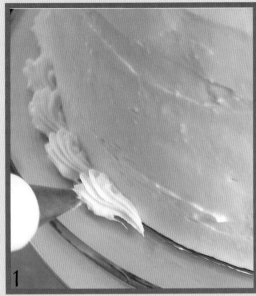

1. Using pastry bags and desired tips, decorate the cake starting with the bottom border.

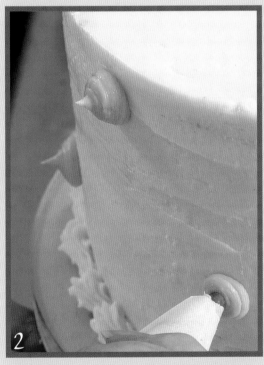

2. Continue with side decorations then top decorations. *Note: Writing should be last.*

3. Step back to view cake. If necessary, add additional decorations. *Note: This cake was decorated with several pastry bags, each filled with a different color. Round tips in various sizes were used for the piping.*

The above cake was decorated with chopped nuts. A Buttercream Icing border was then piped around the top edge.

6
technique

Equipment:
Measuring cups: dry; liquid
Microwavable bowl
Microwave
Wire whisk

Ganache:
Heavy whipping cream
Dark chocolate chips

Note: Use 2 parts chocolate to 1 part heavy whipping cream.

TIPS:

• Use Ganache as filling between cake layers by whipping Ganache until mixture has cooled and is light and fluffy. Do not overwhip.

• Make certain Ganache is thick enough to hold its shape before piping.

• Flavor Ganache with extracts and liqueurs.

How do I make ganache?

Ganache is a rich mixture made from two parts dark chocolate and one part heavy whipping cream. Ganache can be made in large or small amounts. Because of the chocolate in ganache, it is normal for the consistency to set up while icing a cake. However, ganache can be easily warmed again for a thinner consistency. Ganache also can be piped onto cakes, creating borders and lettering.

Ganache—*Here's How:*

MAKING

1. Heat heavy whipping cream to scalding in the microwave. Add room-temperature chocolate chips to whipping cream.

2. Using wire whisk, fold chocolate chips into whipping cream until melted, making certain there are no lumps.

- Ganache that has set up or cooled works well to ice a cake.

- Ganache that is still warm works well to drizzle or pour over a cake. If Ganache needs to be warmed place in a sink filled with hot water.

- Fruit, pretzels, or candy can be dipped into any remaining Ganache.

Equipment:
Airtight container
Heavy aluminum saucepan
Large metal spoon
Measuring cup: liquid
Measuring spoons
Mixer w/bowl
Stovetop
Wire whisk

Fondant:

2 pounds powdered sugar
5 teaspoons powdered gelatin
¼ cup water
½ cup corn syrup
1½ tablespoons glycerin

How do I make fondant?

Fondant is made from a few simple ingredients, mostly powdered sugar. Fondant can be molded, rolled, and shaped. Fondant produces a soft molded finish that is easy to cut and does not splinter. It is applied to a cake in one large piece. Fondant is easy to make, but does take some practice to learn how to apply to a cake. Fondant can be tinted with food coloring during kneading process, or it can be painted with food coloring after it has been applied to a cake. It also can be flavored during the kneading process. Excess fondant can be stored for two weeks in an airtight container in the refrigerator.

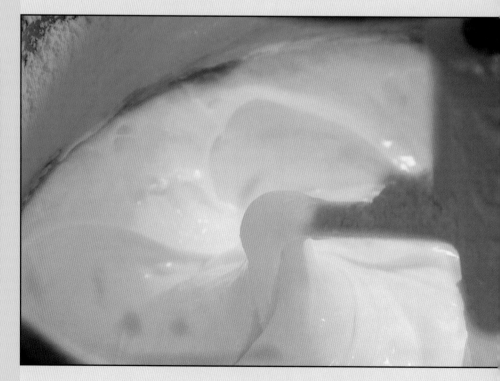

Fondant—*Here's How:*

MAKING

1. For the blooming process, stir gelatin and water together in saucepan. Allow mixture to bloom for three minutes. *Note: The process called blooming makes the mixture easier to stir and mix.*

2. Stir in corn syrup and glycerin. Heat on medium until gelatin is completely dissolved, stirring constantly or mixture will scorch.

3. Combine gelatin mixture and powdered-sugar mixture together in mixing bowl. *Note: Add all powdered sugar at once if consistency in mixer will allow. If not, finish fondant by kneading mixture into remaining powdered sugar on work surface. See photo 3b.*

4. After fondant is completely mixed, place in airtight container overnight.

technique

Equipment:
Airtight container
Heavy aluminum saucepan
Measuring cup: liquid
Measuring spoons
Mixer w/bowl and paddle
Mixing bowl
Powdered sugar
Spray bottle w/water
Stovetop
Wire whisk

Gum Paste:

1 package gelatin
¼ cup water
1 tablespoon light corn syrup
1 pound powdered sugar

How do I make gum paste?

Gum paste is pliable, easy to shape, and versatile. The batch of gum paste can be tinted or divided into several portions and tinted different colors. When creating decorative items from gum paste, make plenty. Gum paste can be used to make a variety of cake decorations such as bows, flowers, and ribbons. They keep for 12 months and are easy to store in an airtight container. If you do not tint the batch of gum paste, do not paint decorative gum-paste items until using them to decorate a cake. This way the decorative items can be painted to match the individual cake.

Gum Paste—*Here's How:*

MAKING

1. Stir gelatin and water together in saucepan. Allow mixture to bloom for three minutes.

2. Stir in corn syrup. Heat on medium until gelatin is completely dissolved, stirring constantly or the mixture will scorch.

3. In mixing bowl, alternate gelatin mixture with powdered sugar and mix until stiff. Keep gum paste covered with plastic wrap to keep moist or store in airtight container.

TIPS:

- Gum Paste can be kept in an airtight container for up to four days.

- Gum Paste can be dyed with food coloring, which is best when making certain decorative items such as roses.

The following text on pages 48–55 explains how to create various florals from Gum Paste as shown at right and below. *Note: Before working with Gum Paste, a work surface must be prepared.*

Lily & Leaf on pages 48–49

Buds on page 50

Sweet Pea on page 51

Dogwood on pages 52–54

Rose on pages 54–55

PREPARING WORK SURFACE

1. Prepare work surface, using the following method:

a. Using spray bottle, spray the work surface with water.

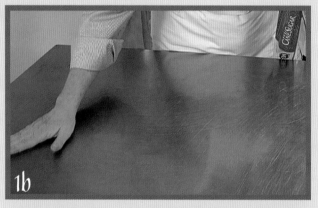

b. Using hand, spread water on work surface.

c. Pour a generous amount of powdered sugar onto work surface. Using hand, spread the powered sugar.

2. Allow powdered sugar to stand for five minutes.

MAKING LILIES & LEAVES

1. Spread a layer of granular sugar on baking sheet.

2. Using wire cutters, cut five 4" wires. Using needle-nosed pliers, bend one end of each wire, creating a hook.

3. Using rolling pin, roll out gum paste to ¹⁄₁₆" on work surface.

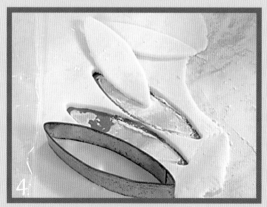

4. Using leaf cutter, cut eight leaf shapes from gum paste.

5. Using tulip press, press five shapes, creating petals. Using leaf mold, press remaining shapes, creating vein impressions in leaves.

6. Wrap one end of each petal around wire hook, making certain wire is surrounded with gum paste. Pinch. If necessary, reshape petal. Lay in granular sugar on baking sheet to dry.

7. Place petals and leaves in airtight container until you are ready to paint and apply to finished cake.

This airtight container holds sweet peas that have been made from untinted Gum Paste and dyed Gum Paste. Gum Paste can be dyed to desired tint while mixing.

MAKING BUDS

1. Using wire cutters, cut desired number of 4" wire lengths. Using needle-nosed pliers, bend one end of each wire, creating a hook.

2. Coat hands with powdered sugar.

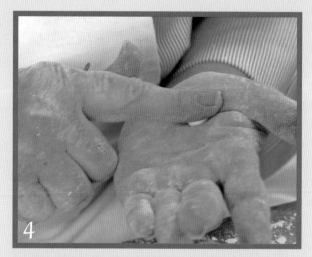

4. Finger-press gum paste in palm of hand.

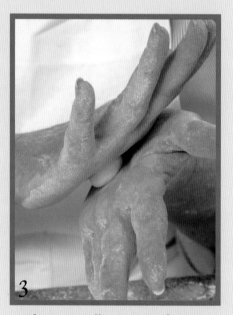

3. Place a small amount of gum paste in your hand and roll until soft and pliable. *Note: If gum paste gets too soft, place powdered sugar on your fingertips. This helps dry the gum paste. If the gum paste gets too dry and begins to crack, warm with your hand until the consistency softens.*

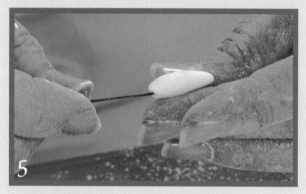

5. Wrap gum paste around wire hook, creating a bud.

6. Insert wired bud into Styrofoam sheet. Allow to dry overnight.

7. Place buds in airtight container until you are ready to paint and apply to finished cake.

Additional Equipment:
Airtight container
Circle cutters: 1"; 1½"
Florist tape
Needle-nosed pliers
Rolling pin
Styrofoam® sheet
Wire: 24 gauge
Wire cutters

6. Finger-press around edge to thin.

MAKING SWEET PEAS

1. Using wire cutters, cut desired number of 4" wire lengths. Using needle-nosed pliers, bend one end of each, creating a hook.

2. Make one bud for each sweet pea. Refer to Making Buds on page 50.

3. Prepare work surface. Refer to Preparing Work Surface, Steps 1–2 on page 48.

4. Using rolling pin, roll out gum paste to ⅟₁₆" on work surface.

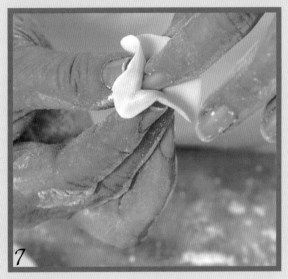

7. Pinch together at center of circle, creating sweet pea.

8. Press wire hook into bottom of sweet pea, making certain wire is surrounded with gum paste. Pinch.

9. Insert wire into Styrofoam sheet. Allow to dry overnight.

5. Using circle cutters, cut out circle shapes in two different sizes for small and large sweet peas.

10. Place one large sweet pea, one small sweet pea, and one bud together to achieve desired look.

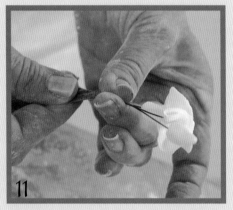

11. Tape wire ends together with florist tape.

12. Place petals and leaves in air-tight container until you are ready to paint and apply to finished cake.

MAKING DOGWOOD

1. Prepare work surface. Refer to Preparing Work Surface, Steps 1–2 on page 48.

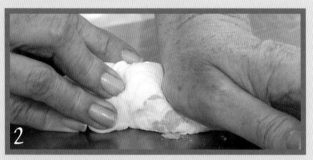

2. Knead yellow food coloring into small portion of gum paste.

3. Using small pastry brush, brush press with powdered sugar.

4. Press grape-sized piece of gum paste into dogwood-center mold. Flex dogwood center from mold.

5. Wrap dogwood center onto toothpick.

6. Insert in Styrofoam sheet. Allow to dry overnight.

7. Spread a layer of granular sugar on baking sheet.

8. Using rolling pin, roll out gum paste to ⅟₁₆" on work surface.

9. Using dogwood cutter, cut dogwood petals. Set aside and cover with plastic wrap.

10. Using 2"-wide pastry brush, brush dogwood press with powdered sugar.

11. Press dogwood petals, creating vein impressions. Using toothpick, poke a hole in center of flower.

12. Lay in granular sugar on baking sheet. Allow petals to partially dry. Reshape dogwood petals into a flower. *Note: Dogwood petals can be finger-pressed to thin and curl the edges. Each dogwood flower will be unique, depending on whether or not the petals are thinned, pressed inward toward the center, or simply left flat.*

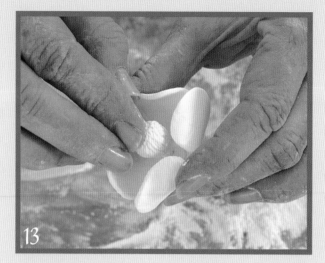

13. Insert dry dogwood center into the center of the dry flower.

14. Place petals and leaves in airtight container until you are ready to paint and apply to the finished cake.

Cupcakes can be made from most cake recipes. Most decorating techniques that can be applied to a cake can be applied to a cupcake. The photo above shows cupcakes that have been decorated with Gum-paste florals. Dogwood petals have been painted with food coloring and a dab of yellow icing has been added to the center. A painted Gum-paste leaf has been added for an extra splash of color.

Additional Equipment:
Craft scissors

MAKING ROSES

1. Lightly coat hands with powdered sugar.

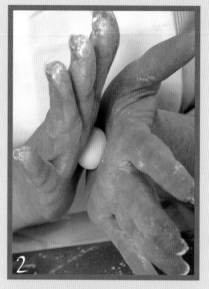

2. Place a small amount of gum paste in your hand and roll until soft and pliable.

3. Using two fingers and thumbs, form rose base.

4. Press grape-sized amount of gum paste in your palm. Using fingers, make gum paste round and flat. Finger-press edge to thin for a delicate rose petal.

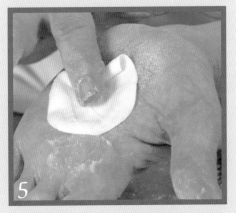

5. Place rose petal in center of palm and begin rolling from edge for a rose center.

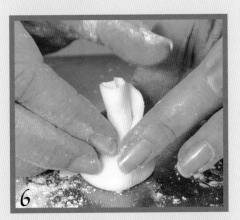

6. Secure rose petal onto rose base.

7. Repeat Steps 4–6 for each petal, making each petal slightly larger until desired look is achieved. *Note: Each rose is unique depending on how many petals are added.*

8. Using fingers and thumbs, open up rose by pressing in at base until achieving desired look. *Note: It takes about five minutes to make a rose. Work quickly so gum paste stays pliable when adding petals.*

9. Allow to dry overnight.

10. Using scissors, trim off excess base.

11. Place roses in airtight container until you are ready to paint and apply to finished cake.

Section 3: Beyond the Basics

1
project

Equipment:
Baking sheet
Cake plate
Decorating tips
Food coloring: green; pink
Measuring cups: dry; liquid
Measuring spoons
Metal spatula
Mixer w/bowl
Mixing bowls
Oven
Pastry bags
Rectangular cake pan:
13" x 9"
Serrated-edged knife
Sifter
Wire whisk

Petit Four Toppings:
Coconut
Chopped nuts

How do I decorate petit fours?

Petit fours are tiny iced cakes. These petit fours have been rolled in coconut and chopped nuts. A rosebud has been added to the top for that extra special touch. Petit fours can also be decorated with fondant and/or gum-paste florals. You could design a custom petit four for each guest at your dinner party. Use your creativity and have fun.

Petit Fours—*Here's How:*

MAKING & BAKING

1. Make and bake a 13" x 9" Italian Cream Cake. See Italian Cream Cake at right.

2. Cool cake completely. Remove from pan and place on work surface.

3. Make Buttercream Icing. See Buttercream Icing on page 27. *Note: Make certain icing is thin so it will not tear cake. Add a drop or two of water to thin icing.*

DECORATING

1. Using serrated-edged knife, cut 2"-sq. petit fours from cake.

2. Combine food coloring and one tablespoon of water to make desired tint. Using fingers, blend color into coconut.

Italian Cream Cake:

1 cup buttermilk

1 teaspoon baking soda

5 eggs, separated

2 cups sugar

½ cup shortening

½ cup butter

2 cups sifted flour

1 teaspoon vanilla extract

MAKING & BAKING

1. Preheat oven to 325°.

2. Stir buttermilk and soda together in mixing bowl. Let stand. In mixer, beat egg whites until stiff. Set aside.

3. In mixer, cream together sugar, butter, shortening, and egg yolks.

4. Add buttermilk mixture to sugar mixture. Alternate, adding flour and vanilla to batter. Mix together. Place batter in mixing bowl.

5. Using whisk, fold in egg whites. Bake for 30 minutes. Using thin-edged knife, test center of cake. Remove cake from oven when knife comes clean.

59

3. Using metal spatula, place icing on four sides of petit four.

4. Roll sides in coconut. Place on baking sheet.

Note: Sides can also be rolled in chopped nuts.

5. Apply icing to top of petit four.

6. Place a small amount of icing into two separate mixing bowls. Color the icing in one bowl pink and in the other bowl green. Refer to For Colored Icing on page 29.

TIP:

- After removing baking sheet from oven, allow to cool. Place baking sheet in freezer for forty-five minutes. This will tighten the crumbs on the cake and make it easier to cut.

7. Using pastry bag and desired decorating tip, decorate petit fours. Refer to Using Pastry Bag & Tips Steps 1–4 on page 39.

Beautifully decorated petit fours make ideal place-setting treats for any special occasion. Ice them with seasonal or event motifs using tiny gum-paste florals and piped leaves. Accent with narrow icing, satin, or metallic ribbons.

How do I decorate a bundt cake?

A bundt cake can be beautiful, decorated with a simple glaze and sugared fruit. Sugared fruits are decorative whether fully or partially sugared. Edible flowers can also be sugared and used as decoration. Consult a florist for which flowers are edible, or purchase grocery-flower produce package.

2
project

Equipment:
Bundt pan
Cooling rack
Fresh fruit: not completely ripe
Paper towels
Superfine sugar
Tablespoon
Water
Wire whisk

Equipment for Chocolate Cake
on page 22

Bundt Cake—*Here's How:*

MAKING & BAKING

1. Make and bake a bundt cake. See Chocolate Cake on page 23. Refer to Technique 1, Steps 1–13 on pages 22–24.

2. Cool cake completely. Using thin-edged knife, remove bundt cake from pan by running knife around edges of cake pan. Make certain to avoid cutting the cakes. *Note: The natural edge on the cakes helps them hold their shape and makes it much easier to ice.*

3. Make Egg Mixture. See Egg Mixture on page 63.

4. Make Glaze. See Glaze on page 63.

SUGARING FRESH FRUIT

1. Rinse and dry all fruit.

2. Pour superfine sugar into a mixing bowl.

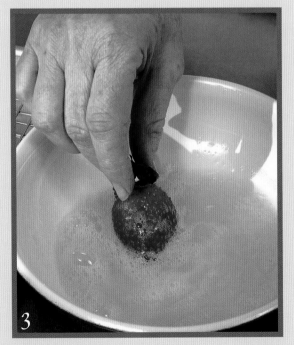

3. Dip desired fresh fruit into Egg Mixture.

4. Roll dipped fruit in sugar.

5. Place fruit on cooling rack. Allow to dry for four hours.

62

DECORATING

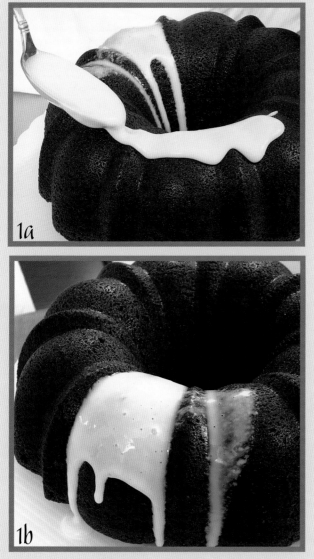

1a

1b

1. Using tablespoon, pour Glaze onto top of bundt cake, allowing Glaze to drip down sides. *Note: If Glaze is too runny, simply add more powdered sugar to glaze and whip. See comparison in photo 1b.*

2. Garnish bundt cake with sugared fruit.

Glaze:

¼ cup orange juice
2 cups powdered sugar

MIXING

1. In mixing bowl, combine ingredients.

2. Using wire whisk, whip glaze to desired thickness.

Egg Mixture:

4 ounces pasteurized egg whites
1 teaspoon salt

MIXING

1. In mixing bowl, combine ingredients. *Note: Beating in salt aids in breaking down the egg whites.*

2. Using wire whisk, whip egg white mixture.

3
project

Equipment:
Cake plate
Dish towel
Flour
Jelly cake-roll pan: 16½" x 11½"
Measuring spoons
Metal spatula
Mixing bowl
Mixer w/bowl
Oven
Refrigerator
Rubber spatula
Shortening
Sifter
Thin-edged knife
Waxed paper
Wooden spoon

Equipment for Ganache
on page 42

Chocolate Cake Roll:

10 eggs
1 cup powdered sugar
6 tablespoons cocoa
1 cup powdered sugar
1 tablespoon salt
¼ cup flour
Strawberries

How do I make and decorate a chocolate cake roll?

A cake roll is a cake rolled around a filling. The cake of a cake roll can be made in any desired flavor and can be filled with a variety of fillings from whipped cream, to fruit, to ice cream. The cake roll is rolled twice, once to prepare it for the filling and again with the filling added.

Chocolate Cake Roll—*Here's How:*

MAKING & BAKING

1. Preheat oven to 350°. Grease bottom of pan with shortening.

2. Place waxed paper on the prepared pan.

3. Flour waxed paper. Holding pan upside down, tap out excess flour.

4. Sift dry ingredients onto waxed paper on work surface.

5. Separate egg yolks from whites. Beat egg whites until stiff.

6. Pour dry ingredients into yolks and stir using wooden spoon.

7. Place ¼ of egg whites in batter. Using wooden spoon, fold mixture together.

8. Using wire whisk, fold in remaining egg whites.

9. Pour and spread batter in pan. Bake for 12 minutes. Test cake with thin-edged knife before removing from oven. Make certain knife comes out clean.

10. Cool cake in pan for 15 minutes or until cool to touch.

11. Make Whipped Cream. See Whipped Cream on page 67.

12. Make Ganache. See Ganache on page 42. Refer to Technique 6, Steps 1–2 on page 43.

ASSEMBLING

1. Sift the powdered sugar onto the clean dish towel.

2. Flip cake onto dish towel. Carefully remove pan.

3. Remove waxed paper from cake.

4. Using dish towel, roll cake to prepare for filling. Cool in refrigerator for 30 minutes.

5. Place on cake plate and unroll. Remove dish towel.

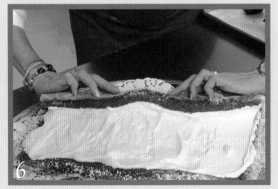

6. Using metal spatula, spread whipped cream onto cake and roll.

7. Roll up cake completely.

Note: Whipped Cream may squeeze out the ends and sides. This simply adds to its appeal.

DECORATING

1. Using metal spatula, ice Chocolate Cake Roll with Ganache. Dip strawberries in remaining ganache for garnish.

TIPS:

• While whipping cream, gradually increase the speed of the mixer from low to high to cut down on the powdered sugar dust that may get all over you and your work space.

• While whipping cream, drape a clean dish towel over the mixer to cut down on the powdered sugar dust. Make certain the dish towel is large enough to drape over the sides of the mixer bowl without getting caught in the mixer.

• Use powdered sugar instead of granular sugar to help the whipped cream hold its shape.

Whipped Cream:

1 pint heavy whipping cream
1 cup powdered sugar
1 teaspoon vanilla

MIXING

1. Mix heavy whipping cream and powdered sugar together.

2. Add vanilla. Mix until light and fluffy.

4
project

Equipment:
Fine-tipped paintbrush
Floral craft stamen
Florist tape
Food coloring:
burgundy; green
Pastry bag
Serrated-edged knife
Soft-bristled paintbrush:
medium
Square cake pans: 8" (2)
Ramekins
Water

Equipment for Chocolate
Cake on page 22

Equipment for Iced Cake
on page 27

Equipment for Ganache
on page 43

Equipment for Gum Paste
on page 47

How do I decorate a cake with ganache and gum-paste florals?

Ganache can be used in various ways—icing, filling, piped or drizzled onto a cake. The cake shown below is decorated with ganache icing. The cake is then drizzled with ganache and embellished with a painted gum-paste floral.

Ganache Lily Cake—*Here's How:*

MAKING & BAKING

1. Make Gum-paste lilies and leaves. Refer to Making Lilies & Leaves, Steps 1–6 on pages 48–49.

2. Make and bake two 8" Chocolate Cakes. See Chocolate Cake on page 23. Refer to Technique 1, Steps 1–13 on pages 22–24.

3. Make Buttercream Icing. See Buttercream Icing on page 27.

4. Make Raspberry Filling. See Raspberry Filling on page 71.

5. Make Ganache. See Ganache on page 42. Refer to Technique 6, Steps 1–2 on page 43.

HAND-PAINTING LILIES & LEAVES

1. Mix small amount of water and burgundy food coloring to light tint in a ramekin.

3. Surround stamen with petals.

4. Using florist tape, secure stamen and petals together.

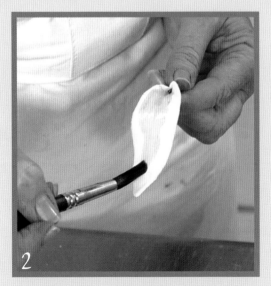

2. Using medium-bristled paintbrush, apply color to center of each petal. Blend color to the edge of petal with water.

5. Using fine-tipped paintbrush and burgundy food coloring, add details on lily as desired.

6. Set lily aside to dry.

7. Mix small amount of water and green food coloring to the desired tint in a ramekin.

8. Using medium-bristled paintbrush, apply color to center of leaves. Blend color to edge of leaves with water.

9. Set leaves aside to dry.

ASSEMBLING

1. Using serrated-edged knife, remove any high spots and level off top. *Note: Be careful to not remove too much. You can always go back and remove more if necessary.* Place cake on cake plate.

2. Place Buttercream Icing in pastry bag. Refer to Assembling Pastry Bag, Steps 1–4 and 6–10 on pages 37–38. Using decorating bag without a tip, make a dam around top of one cake.

3. Fill area inside dam with raspberry filling. Do not place too much filling inside dam or it will leak out and be difficult to ice.

4. Place remaining cake upside down on filling.

5. Brush off excess crumbs.

ASSEMBLING

1. Crumb-coat cake with Ganache. Refer to Crumb Coating, Steps 1–2 on page 28.

2. Using metal spatula, ice cake with Ganache. Make certain Ganache has cooled to icing consistency. If necessary, place in refrigerator until it thickens slightly.

3. Place container with remaining Ganache in a sink of water to reach pouring consistency. Pour Ganache onto top center of cake.

4. Using metal spatula, spread Ganache, allowing it to drip down sides.

Raspberry Filling:

10 ounces frozen raspberries
1 tablespoon cornstarch
½ cup currant jelly

MIXING

1. Thaw raspberries. Using hand, crush raspberries while still in sealed bag.

2. Place raspberries in saucepan with cornstarch and jelly. Cook over medium heat, stirring constantly until bubbly. Cook an additional minute. Allow to cool.

5. Insert lily into cake.

6. Add leaves as desired.

How do I decorate a simple fondant-iced cake?

The cake below was created by covering three 8" cakes that were each 3" high with fondant. A fondant-iced cake makes any occasion special, for example a child's first birthday. The fondant has been painted with food coloring and the child's first words have been piped onto the cake.

Equipment:
Candle: 8"
Decorating tips
Food coloring: green; pink
Medium-bristled paintbrushes
Microwave
Pastry bag
Pizza cutter
Ramekins
Rolling pin
Round cake pans: 8" (3)
Smoother
Spray bottle w/water
Tape measure
Water

Equipment for Chocolate Cake
on page 22

Equipment for Fondant
on page 44

Fondant-iced
Cake——*Here's How:*

MAKING & BAKING

1. Make and bake three 8" Chocolate Cakes. See Chocolate Cake on page 23. Refer to Technique 1, Steps 1–13 on pages 22–24.

2. Make Fondant. See Fondant on page 44. Refer to Technique 7, Steps 1–4 on page 45.

3. Make Buttercream Icing. See Buttercream Icing on page 27.

4. Crumb-coat cake. Refer to Crumb Coating, Steps 1–2 on page 28.

KNEADING & ROLLING FONDANT

1. Prepare work surface. Refer to Preparing Work Surface, Steps 1–2 on page 48.

2. Warm Fondant in microwave for one minute. Take Fondant out of microwave. Remove any Fondant that is soft and place on work surface. Return remaining Fondant to microwave. Warm for one minute. Take Fondant out of microwave. Remove any Fondant that is soft and place on work surface. Repeat process until all Fondant is soft.

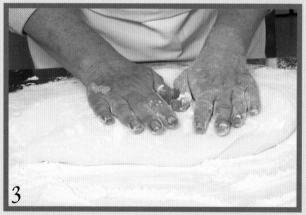

3. Knead Fondant.

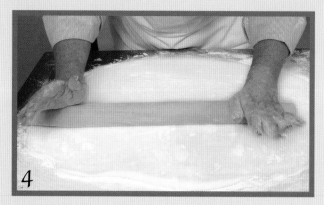

4. Using rolling pin, roll out Fondant in all directions to make round. *Note: Be aware of length and width of the cake. Use tape measure to measure cake. Sometimes in order to get the necessary length to cover the cake, you come up short on the width (sides).*

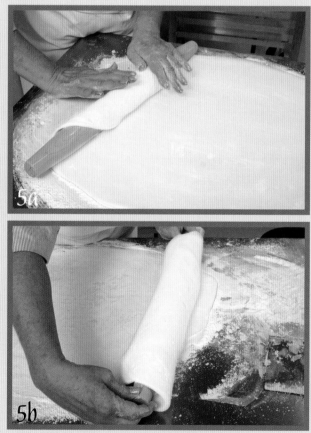

5. Roll Fondant onto rolling pin.

6. Roll Fondant onto cake, starting on farthest side, working toward you.

FITTING FONDANT TO CAKE

1. Fit Fondant to cake. Using right hand, pull the Fondant down while contouring Fondant to cake with left hand.

2. Using pizza cutter, trim off excess.

3. Remove excess Fondant from cake.

4. Using smoother, smooth Fondant in a circular motion.

5. Using hands, make a clean uniform edge all the way around top of cake. *Note: If design calls for a rounded edge, use hands to make rounded edge uniform.*

TIPS:

- For flawless Fondant, make certain the work surface, rolling pin, smoother, and hands are clean and lint-free.

- If you run out of powdered sugar when preparing the work surface, cornstarch can be used on the work surface and your hands.

- To determine needed amount of rolled Fondant, add the diameter of the cake to double the height of the assembled cake for the total. In powdered sugar, draw the total measurement in a circle on work surface with fingertip. Roll Fondant out to match this circle.

- Make certain to roll Fondant out to ¼" thickness. If rolled thinner, the cake imperfections will show through.

DECORATING

1. Mix a small amount of water and pink food coloring in a ramekin to create desired tint.

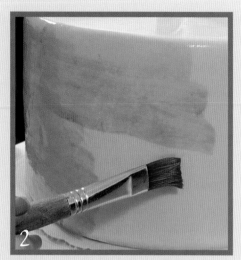

2. Using medium-bristled paint-brush, apply food coloring to cake, stroking horizontally until entire cake is covered. *Note: This technique leaves brush marks. If you do not wish to see the brush strokes, add food coloring to Fondant while mixing or knead color into Fondant.*

3. Using pastry bag and decorating tip, decorate bottom edge of cake with Buttercream Icing. Refer to Using Pastry Bags & Tips, Steps 1–3 on page 40.

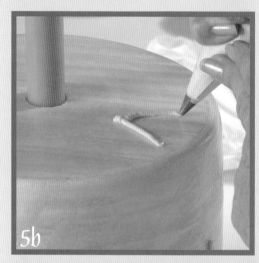

4. Insert candle into center of cake.

5. Using pastry bag and decorating tips, randomly decorate cake with baby's first words, with Buttercream Icing.

How do I decorate fondant-iced cakes with gum-paste florals and twigs?

What makes these fondant-iced cakes unique are the floral designs which were hand-painted onto the fondant before the ribbon, gum-paste florals, and twigs were added. It only takes some paintbrushes, food coloring, and your creative strokes. Practice the design on a scrap of fondant before painting directly onto the fondant-iced cake.

6 project

Equipment:
Cake plates (3)
Cooling rack
Decorating tips
Drinking glass
Food coloring: assorted colors
Pastry bag
Pizza cutter
Ramekins
Ribbon: 1½"-wide
Rolling pin
Round cake pans:
6" (2); 9" (2); 12" (2)
Smoother
Soft-bristled paintbrushes:
assorted
Spray bottle w/water
Styrofoam® sheet
Twigs

Equipment for Chocolate Cake
on page 22

Equipment for Fondant on
page 44

Equipment for Gum Paste
on page 46

Royal Icing:

2 pounds powdered sugar
5 tablespoons meringue powder
½ teaspoon cream of tartar
1 cup water

MIXING

1. Mix water, meringue, cream of tartar until frothy. Add powdered sugar.

2. Apply icing to cake to attach Gum-paste florals, candy, etc.

TIP:

• Since only a small amount of Royal Icing will be used at one time, separate 1½ to 2 cups of icing into plastic sandwich bags. Keep refrigerated. To use, place contents of plastic sandwich bag into a mixing bowl. Beat until stiff and fluffy.

Fondant & Gum-paste Floral Cake—*Here's How:*

MAKING & BAKING

1. Make Gum Paste. See Gum Paste on page 46. Make buds, leaves, lilies, roses, and sweet peas. Refer to Technique 8 on pages 47–55.

2. Make and bake two 6", two 9", and two 12" Chocolate Cakes. See Chocolate Cake on page 23. Refer to Technique 1, Steps 1–13 on pages 22–24

3. Make Fondant. See Fondant on page 44. Refer to Technique 7, Steps 1–4 on page 45.

4. Make Royal Icing at left.

5. Make Buttercream Icing. See Buttercream Icing on page 27.

6. Crumb-coat cake. Refer to Crumb Coating, Steps 1–2 on page 28.

7. Smooth-ice cake. Refer to For Smooth Icing, Steps 1–2 on page 30.

HAND-PAINTING LILIES & LEAVES

1. Hand-paint three lilies and desired number of leaves. Refer to Project 4, Steps 1–9 on pages 69–70.

DIP-PAINTING SWEET PEAS

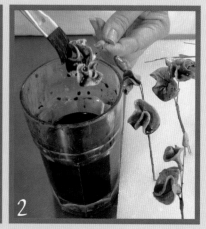

1. Place purple food coloring in an old drinking glass. Dip sweet peas into glass.

2. If necessary, use soft-bristled paintbrush to touch up sweet pea as desired. Insert into Styrofoam to dry.

HAND-PAINTING ROSES

1. Place desired food coloring in a ramekin.

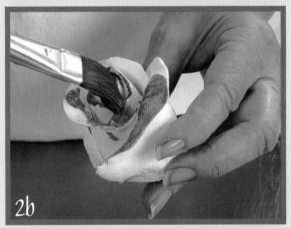

2. Using soft-bristled paintbrush, paint roses.

3. Place on cooling rack. Allow to dry.

HAND-PAINTING DOGWOOD

1. Place desired food coloring in a ramekin.

2. Using soft-bristled paintbrush, paint dogwood as desired.

3. Insert in Styrofoam to dry.

KNEADING & ROLLING FONDANT

1. Prepare work surface. Refer to Preparing Work Surface, Steps 1–2 on page 48.

2. Knead and roll Fondant. Refer to Kneading & Rolling Fondant, Steps 1–5 on page 74.

3. Fit Fondant to cakes. Refer to Fitting Fondant to Cake, Steps 1–5 on page 75.

DECORATING

1. Mix a small amount of water and food coloring in ramekin to create desired tint. Paint Fondant with food coloring.

2. Using medium-bristled paintbrush, apply food coloring to cake, stroking horizontally until entire cake is covered.

3. Wrap ribbon around bottom of cake. Secure with a dab of Royal Icing. *Note: Ribbon or icing borders are used to hide imperfections on Fondant edges.*

4. Using desired paintbrushes and food coloring, practice painting desired floral design on paper or extra Fondant first. *Note: By practicing on Fondant you learn how your paintbrush will release color.*

5a

5b

5. Apply food coloring in desired design on cake.

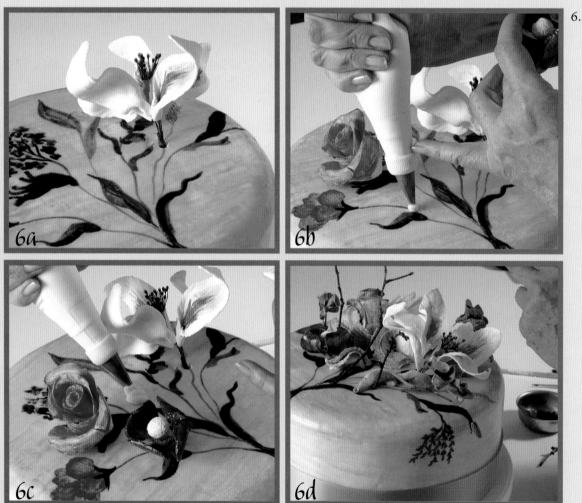

6a

6b

6c

6d

6. Using pastry bag and decorating tips, place a small dab of Royal Icing where florals will be placed. Insert Gumpaste florals and twigs in cake as desired.

How do I make a sculpted cake?

Sculpted cakes are made by stacking cakes and trimming them into a desired shape. The duck cake shown below was created from three different-sized oval cakes. The cakes were layered, sculpted, and covered with fondant to create a duck. The duck head and beak were created using Styrofoam® shapes. The duck has been placed on an acrylic cake plate and placed in a blue fabric "water" setting.

Equipment:
Butter knife
Cake plate
Dowel: ½" dia.
Food coloring: black; orange; yellow
Metal spatula
Oval cake pans:
8"; 11" (2); 13½"
Paintbrushes: assorted sizes
Paring knife
Pastry bag
Pizza cutter
Powdered sugar
Ramekins
Rolling pin
Serrated-edged knife
Shortening
Smoother
Spray bottle w/water
Stovetop/oven
Styrofoam® forms:
5" dia. ball; 7" egg; sheet
Tape measure
Toothpicks
Water
Wooden spoon

Equipment for Iced Cake
on page 27

Equipment for Fondant
on page 44

Sculpted Duck Cake—*Here's How:*

MAKING & BAKING

Note: Fondant on duck beak and duck head will need to dry overnight, so cake baking should be done on the second day.

1. Make and bake one 8", two 11", and one 13½" Italian Cream Cakes. See Italian Cream Cake on page 59.

2. Make Buttercream Icing. See Buttercream Icing on page 27.

3. Make Royal Icing. See Royal Icing on page 78.

4. Make Raspberry Filling. See Raspberry Filling on page 71.

5. Make Fondant and knead in yellow food coloring. See Fondant on page 44. Refer to Technique 7, Steps 1–4 on page 45.

ASSEMBLING DUCK'S HEAD

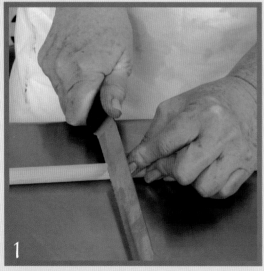

1. Using serrated-edged knife, cut dowel at an angle to 10" length for neck.

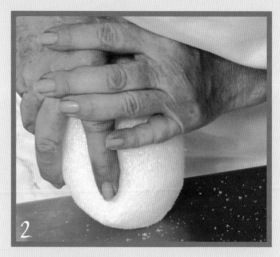

2. Using hands, press small end of Styrofoam egg flat to form beak.

3. Using serrated-edged knife, cut egg in half for beak.

4. Using paring knife, sculpt beak to fit against Styrofoam ball.

5. Prepare work surface. Refer to Preparing Work Surface, Steps 1–2 on page 48.

6. Coat beak with Royal Icing.

7. Using rolling pin, roll out Fondant to ¼" thickness in all directions to make round.

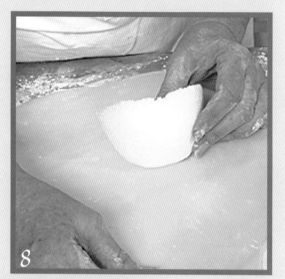

8. Place beak on Fondant. Cover the beak with Fondant.

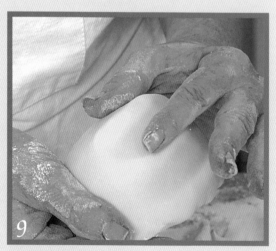

9. Shape beak's edges.

10. Insert toothpicks on inside of beak.

11. Using metal spatula, coat Styrofoam ball with Royal Icing for head.

12. Insert dowel 2" into head for neck.

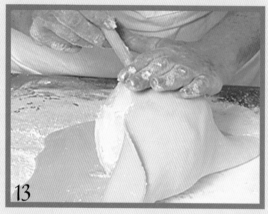

13. Cover head with Fondant.

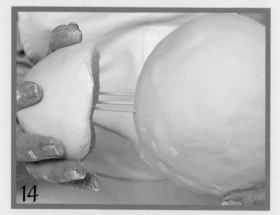

14. Insert beak into head. Using pastry bag, caulk seam with Royal Icing. Refer to Technique 5, Steps 1–4 and 6–10 on pages 37–38. Smooth icing in place with finger.

DECORATING DUCK'S HEAD

1. Insert dowel into Styrofoam sheet to secure while painting.

2. Mix a small amount of water and orange food coloring in a ramekin to create desired tint.

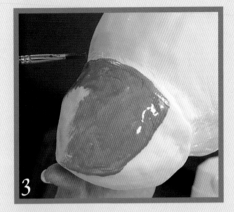

3. Paint beak.

4. Place a small amount of black food coloring in a ramekin.

Paint eyes, eyelashes, and nostrils on beak.

5. Allow to dry overnight.

ASSEMBLING DUCK'S BODY

1. Place 11" cake on cake plate.

2. Place Buttercream Icing in pastry bag. Using decorating bag without a tip, make a dam around top of one cake.

3. Using wooden spoon, fill area inside dam with raspberry filling. *Note: Do not place too much filling inside dam or it will leak out and be difficult to ice.*

4. Place 13½" cake upside down on filling. Repeat Steps 2–3 for Assembling Duck's Body on opposite page.

5. Place 11" cake upside down on filling. Repeat Steps 2–3.

6. Place 8" cake at top.

7. Using serrated-edged knife, shave off the rough edges to sculpt the duck's body.

8. Crumb-coat cake. Refer to Crumb Coating, Steps 1–2 on page 28.

9. Prepare work surface.

10. Using rolling pin, roll out Fondant to ¼" thickness in all directions to make round.

11. Using tape measure, measure duck's body and rolled out Fondant to make certain that you have enough Fondant.

TIPS:
- After sculpting cake, stand back and view. If necessary, sculpt additional sections.

- Avoid using perishable fillings, icings, and decorations on your Fondant-iced cakes, which will need to be refrigerated. The moisture from the refrigerator will create condensation on the cake, causing problems with the Fondant and causing tinted icing to bleed.

- When freezing a Fondant-iced cake, wrap the cake twice—first with plastic wrap, then with aluminum foil.

- Thaw frozen Fondant-iced cakes in their wrappings and, if possible, in an air-conditioned environment. This will cause any condensation to adhere to the wrappers, not to the Fondant.

12. Roll Fondant onto rolling pin.

13. Roll Fondant onto duck's body.

DECORATING

1. Make certain fondant fits cake. Using right hand, pull Fondant down while contouring the Fondant to cake with left hand.

2a.

2b.

2. Using pizza cutter, trim off excess. If necessary, trim again close to edge.

3. Using fingers, form tail by gently pulling up on Fondant.

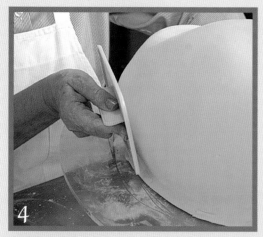

4. Using smoother, smooth surface down to edges.

5. Insert duck's head into duck's body. Make certain angle is as desired before inserting.

6. Using pizza cutter, cut two wings from Fondant as desired.

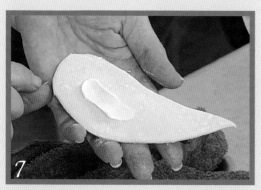

7. Using butter knife, dab a small amount of Royal Icing onto each wing.

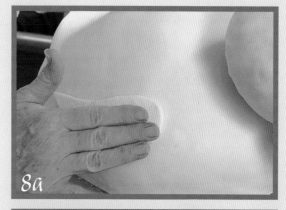

8a

8b

8. Press one wing on each side of duck as desired. *Note: If wings will not stay in place, place toothpicks under each wing for support until it dries.*

Note: The above duck was created with dyed Fondant. The duck on page 81 was also created with dyed Fondant; however, a deeply saturated yellow was desired. So, yellow food coloring was applied to cake with a paintbrush by stroking horizontally until entire cake was covered.

8
project

Equipment:
Cardboard cake rounds:
6"; 9"; 12"
Decorating tips
Dowels: ¼" dia.
Fresh hydrangeas
Handsaw
Large metal spatula
Pastry bag
Powdered sugar
Round cake pans:
12" (2); 9" (2); 6" (2)
Satin ribbon: 1"-wide, cream
Spray bottle w/water
Rolling pin
Smoother
Tape measure

Equipment for Chocolate
Cake on page 22

Equipment for Iced Cake
on page 27

Equipment for Fondant
on page 44

How do I decorate and assemble a tiered cake?

This lovely tiered cake was assembled using dowels which bear the weight of the tiers above. The proper supports, such as dowels, support tubing, cake rounds, and separator plates must be used in the right places in order to keep the cake from toppling over or collapsing.

Three-tiered Cake—*Here's How:*

MAKING & BAKING

1. Make and bake six chocolate cakes. See Chocolate Cake on page 23 and triple the recipe twice.

2. Make Fondant. See Fondant on page 44. Refer to Technique 7, Steps 1–4 on page 45.

3. Make Buttercream Icing. See Buttercream Icing on page 27.

4. Make Royal Icing. See Royal Icing on page 78.

5. Place one of each cake on appropriately sized cardboard cake round (Method 1) or on separator plates (Method 2). Crumb-coat cakes. Refer to Crumb Coating, Steps 1–2 on page 28.

Described are two different methods to prepare cakes for layers. Method 1 is a traditional method, using dowels for the cake's support system. Method 2 uses a patent-pending support system.

PREPARING CAKES FOR TIERS (METHOD 1)

1. Insert ¼" dowel vertically from the top to the plate, into tier. Mark dowel ⅛" above the top of tier. *Note: If not covering cake with Fondant, place dowels flush with cake.*

2. Remove dowel. Using handsaw, cut six dowel pieces to this length.

3. Insert six dowels into bottom tier, forming a circle 2½" from cake edge.

4. Repeat the process, using four dowels for the middle tier. *Note: There are no dowels in the top tier.*

5. Prepare work surface. Refer to Preparing Work Surface, Steps 1–2 on page 48.

6. Using rolling pin, roll out Fondant to ¼" thickness in all directions to make round. Refer to Project 5 on pages 74–75.

7. Roll Fondant onto rolling pin.

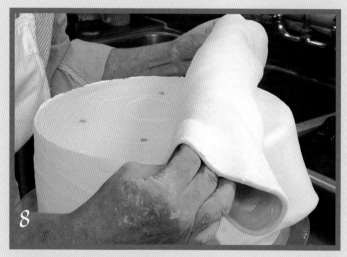

8. Roll Fondant onto bottom tier.

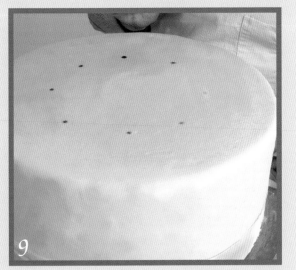

9. Smooth bottom tier with Fondant, allowing the dowels to poke through.

10. Repeat Steps 5–9 on page 89 and above for middle and top tiers.

DECORATING

Note: When transporting a tiered cake it is best to decorate but not assemble the individual tiers before transporting. The tiers can then be assembled at the chosen destination. If necessary, the decorations can be touched up.

1. Wrap ribbon around bottom of each tier. Secure with a dab of Royal Icing. *Note: Ribbon or icing borders are used to hide imperfections on Fondant edges.*

2. Using pastry bag and desired tip, pipe design on each tier. Refer to Technique 5, Steps 1–10 on pages 37–38.

ASSEMBLE TIERS (METHOD 1)

1. Using large metal spatula, center and place middle tier onto top of bottom tier.

2. Center and place top tier onto middle tier, creating a three-tiered cake.

3. Decorate cake with hydrangeas as desired. See photo on page 88.

PREPARING CAKES FOR TIERS (METHOD 2)

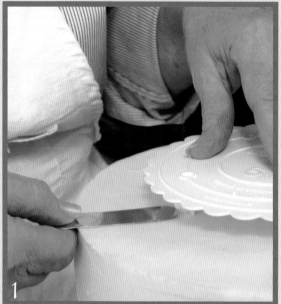

1. Using ruler, center and mark where middle tier will be placed onto top of bottom tier. *Note: It is very important that separator plate is perfectly centered.*

2. Center and insert separator plate into top of bottom tier.

Additional Equipment:
Dowels: ¼" dia.
Paper cutter
Ruler
Separator plates: 6" (1); 9" (1)
Support tubes

3. Remove separator plate.

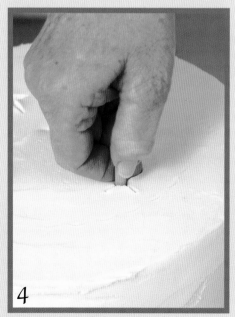

4. Insert dowel into bottom tier to get exact height of tier. Remove.

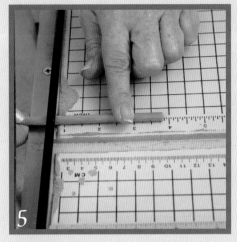

5. Using paper cutter, measure dowel height.

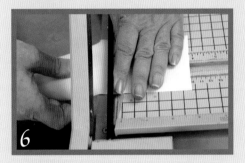

6. Using measurement of dowel as guide, cut four support tubes to height of tier.

7. Insert support tubes into cake, Making certain support tubes go in straight.

ASSEMBLE TIERS (METHOD 2)

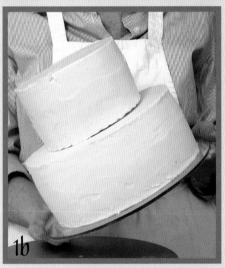

1. Align separator feet with support tubes. Insert feet into tubes. Middle tier is locked in place.

2. Center and place top tier onto middle tier, creating a three-tiered cake. *Note: This method is great because the cake travels in one piece and requires no set-up time at the location.*

The Fondant-iced cake with simple piped-icing designs created in Project 8 can be dramatically altered to suit any taste or any occasion. This three-tiered cake has been embellished four different ways with fresh seasonal florals. The cake was then displayed in a coordinating setting.

The cake in the photo at the left was embellished with mini ranunculus. The cake in the lower-left photo was embellished with bay leaves, then surrounded with silver candleholders and cream-colored candles. The cake in the lower-right photo was embellished with fall leaves, fresh rose petals, and calla lilies, then displayed with items from the autumn harvest.

Section 4: Gallery

My ideas and inspirations for cake decorating come from various sources—bridal magazines, wedding books, advertisements, fabrics, nature, almost everywhere. I take this valuable inspiration and use it, adding my own twist and decorating it slightly differently to make it my own. Various cakes in this gallery have been inspired by wonderful bakers and cake designs.

This cake was created after a bride brought me a photo similar to this cake from a bridal magazine. The technique of painting on a cake with food coloring took me a month to master. However, the entire experience changed the way I decorate cakes. This cake was covered with marzipan, then decorated with hand-painted foliage. Gum-paste fruit embellished each layer. The cake topper consisted of a bird's nest made from marzipan. The birds and the delicate lily placed inside the nest were porcelain from the bride's personal collection. This cake serves 300.

What is a wedding without gifts? This fondant-iced cake was created to resemble gifts of gold and served as the centerpiece for the reception room. The bows were made from gum paste and hand-painted with 24 karat gold paint as were the rest of the gold sections of the cake. This cake serves 200. The individual coordinating cake on the right was created for the bride and groom to take on their honeymoon.

This monochromatic wedding cake was inspired by Martha Stewart. The intricate vines and borders were created from gum paste. The overflowing fruit bowl embellishing the top added to its warm yet elegant look. This cake serves 400.

This four-tiered fondant-iced cake was decorated with delicate leaf designs made from piping with royal icing. The leaves have been filled in with thinned royal icing. The cake topper is a bouquet of gum-paste roses. This cake serves 150.

This multitiered fondant-iced cake was as traditional as wedding cakes come. Each of the nine fondant-iced cakes were embellished with fondant lace. Hand-painted gum-paste florals were tucked into the corners of the bottom tier, while the remaining hand-painted florals were delicately positioned on the other tiers of the cake. This wedding cake serves 350.

This unique wedding cake covered with light blue fondant was created for a winter wedding. The bride and groom wanted their cake to reflect their free spirits while matching their wedding colors—light blue, silver, and white. The top tier of the cake was sculpted to achieve its dome look. Dragées embellished the gum-paste decorations while the curlicue cake topper added the finishing touch. This cake serves 150.

This multitiered cake was created for an outdoor summer wedding. The gum-paste florals embellishing the fondant-iced cake were designed and hand-painted to reflect the florals used to decorate the garden reception and the bridal bouquet. This cake serves 200.

This multitiered wedding cake was created for a garden wedding. Hand-painted vines and flowers decorated each fondant-iced tier, while hand-painted gum-paste florals were delicately placed across the tiers. This wedding cake serves 350.

This all-white multitiered cake featured fondant-iced layers. Each tier was decorated to be distinctively different from the others. The bottom tier was decorated with harlequin-like diamonds of fondant. The middle tier was embellished with three fondant ribbons. The top tier was embellished with piped designs of royal icing. The oversized gum-paste bow cake topper added to its charm. This cake serves 200.

This four-tiered cake was decorated with fondant that was tinted light pink. The lace on the cake was an exact replica of the lace on the bride's dress. The lace was created using #4 round tip and royal icing. Gum-paste flowers were then added as the finishing touch. This cake serves 150.

Each of these cakes was "wrapped" differently with fondant. For cake on the right, the fondant was hand-painted with flowers. For cake on the upper-left, the fondant was lightly tinted. The remaining cake on the left was decorated by piping Royal Icing onto the fondant. All of the cakes are topped with gum-paste bows and ribbon. These cakes serve 100.

This wedding cake featured a multitiered cake resting upon four smaller cakes. The fondant-iced cake was decorated with a fondant border made from a mold. The numerous gum-paste florals were added between the layers. Larger- sized florals were placed into the insets of the scal- loped base to enhance its beauty. This cake serves 200.

This striking multitiered wedding cake was created for a wedding dress designer in New York. The fondant-iced cake featured gum-paste florals that were an exact match to the bride's wedding dress. This cake serves 150.

This four-tier wedding cake was a surprise gift to the bride from her mother. The fondant-iced cake was decorated with gum-paste sweet peas—the bride's favorite flower. A touch of hand-painting further enhanced the cake's beauty. This cake serves 250.

This cake was covered with the palest of pink fondant. Gum-paste grapes and a
gum-paste ribbon were draped onto this elegant cake. Pink tulips accentuated
the layers. This cake serves 100.

About the Author

Jaynie Maxfield baked and decorated her first wedding cake when she was 19 years old. For 30 years, she has been testing recipes, experimenting with colors and textures, and delighting clients in seven states with her stunning, imaginative, often whimsical, and always delicious creations.

Maxfield's fine cakes and her company, Ambrosia Exquisite Wedding Cakes, have been featured in *Utah Bride and Groom* magazine. She has been recognized for her unique sense of style, wit, and especially for her use of color. Her cakes are centerpieces at weddings throughout Utah. She also mentors, teaches, and travels. Mostly, she indulges her passion for the science of baking and the art of cake design. Maxfield resides in Layton, Utah.

Dedication

To my mother who started me on this path with cake pans, a mixer, and fabulous recipes. She praised my ability and let me believe I could do whatever I wanted.

Acknowledgments

The following people/companies have inspired the cakes and the various methods and techniques used in this book.

Cake designer unknown: p. 107
Colette Peters: p. 97
Debra Yates: p. 96
Holly Paulos: p. 93
Jan Kish: p. 98 (r)
Lucinda Larsen
Martha Stewart: pp. 98 (l)
Nordstrom's: p. 103
Polly Schoonmaker: pp. 94 (ur), 94 (lr)
Ron Ben-Israel: pp. 94, 101
Rosemary Watson: p. 99
Sue Green: p. 64
Sugar Bouquets
Wilton Industries, Inc.

Thank-you to Artichoke Company by Holly Paulos. Thank-you to Busath Photographers and Altus Photo Design for their wonderful photography seen on pages 94-108.

A special thank-you to Kevin Dilley of Hazen Photography for his talent, wit, and never-ending charm, and to Karmen Quinney for her hard work, endless questions, and dedication in producing this wonderful book. I could not have done this book without them.

Thank-you to Gracie Brinkerhoff for being such a good model.

For information regarding support tubes, contact:

Ambrosia Exquisite Wedding Cakes
(801) 546-2959
118 South 2625 East
Layton, UT 84040

For information regarding gum-paste cutters and molds:

Sugar Bouquets (800) 203-0629
111 Main Street
Succasunna, NJ 07876
www.sugarbouquets.com

Metric Tables

VOLUME

imperial	equivalent	metric
1 teaspoon [tsp.]		5 ml
3 tsp.	1 [tbsp.]	15 ml
2 tablespoon [tbsp.]	1 fl. oz.	30 ml
1 cup	8 fl. oz.	0.24 litre [l]
2 cups	1 pint [pt.]	0.47 l
4 cups	1 quart [qt.]	0.95 l
4 qts.	1 gallon [gal.]	3.8 l

imperial	UK equivalent	metric
1 fluid ounce [fl. oz.]	1.0408 UK fl. oz.	29.574 ml
1 pt	0.8327 UK pt.	0.4731 l
1 gal.	0.8327 UK gal.	3.7854 l

TEMPERATURE CONVERSION EQUATIONS
degrees Fahrenheit (°F) to degrees Celsius (°C)

$$°F \text{ to } °C = (°F - 32) \times 5/9$$
$$°C \text{ to } °F = (°C \times 9/5) + 32$$

Metric Equivalency Charts

inches to millimetres and centimetres (mm-millimetres   cm-centimetres)

inches	mm	cm	inches	cm	inches	cm	inches	cm
⅛	3	0.3	6	15.2	21	53.3	36	91.4
¼	6	0.6	7	17.8	22	55.9	37	94.0
⅜	10	1.0	8	20.3	23	58.4	38	96.5
½	13	1.3	9	22.9	24	61.0	39	99.1
⅝	16	1.6	10	25.4	25	63.5	40	101.6
¾	19	1.9	11	27.9	26	66.0	41	104.1
⅞	22	2.2	12	30.5	27	68.6	42	106.7
1	25	2.5	13	33.0	28	71.1	43	109.2
1¼	32	3.2	14	35.6	29	73.7	44	111.8
1½	38	3.8	15	38.1	30	76.2	45	114.3
1¾	44	4.4	16	40.6	31	78.7	46	116.8
2	51	5.1	17	43.2	32	81.3	47	119.4
3	76	7.6	18	45.7	33	83.8	48	121.9
4	102	10.2	19	48.3	34	86.4	49	124.5
5	127	12.7	20	50.8	35	88.9	50	127.0

yards to metres

metres	yards	metres	yards	metres	yards	metres	yards	metres	yards
⅛	0.11	2⅛	1.94	4⅛	3.77	6⅛	5.60	8⅛	7.43
¼	0.23	2¼	2.06	4¼	3.89	6¼	5.72	8¼	7.54
⅜	0.34	2⅜	2.17	4⅜	4.00	6⅜	5.83	8⅜	7.66
½	0.46	2½	2.29	4½	4.11	6½	5.94	8½	7.77
⅝	0.57	2⅝	2.40	4⅝	4.23	6⅝	6.06	8⅝	7.89
¾	0.69	2¾	2.51	4¾	4.34	6¾	6.17	8¾	8.00
⅞	0.80	2⅞	2.63	4⅞	4.46	6⅞	6.29	8⅞	8.12
1	0.91	3	2.74	5	4.57	7	6.40	9	8.23
1⅛	1.03	3⅛	2.86	5⅛	4.69	7⅛	6.52	9⅛	8.34
1¼	1.14	3¼	2.97	5¼	4.80	7¼	6.63	9¼	8.46
1⅜	1.26	3⅜	3.09	5⅜	4.91	7⅜	6.74	9⅜	8.57
1½	1.37	3½	3.20	5½	5.03	7½	6.86	9½	8.69
1⅝	1.49	3⅝	3.31	5⅝	5.14	7⅝	6.97	9⅝	8.80
1¾	1.60	3¾	3.43	5¾	5.26	7¾	7.09	9¾	8.92
1⅞	1.71	3⅞	3.54	5⅞	5.37	7⅞	7.20	9⅞	9.03
2	1.83	4	3.66	6	5.49	8	7.32	10	9.14

Index